☐ NATIONAL GEOGRAPHIC SOCIETY

DESTINATION
Rocky Mountains

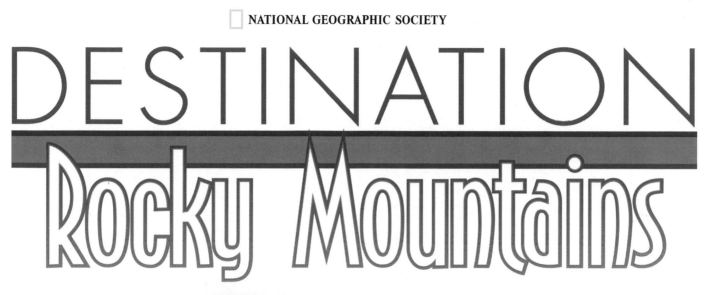

BY JONATHAN GRUPPER

NATIONAL GEOGRAPHIC SOCIETY
WASHINGTON, D.C.

Imagine if you could take wing. If you could soar above the mountaintops. Just imagine what you would see...

They would stretch below you for 2,000 miles—from the southern United States, all the way north into Canada. On and on the mountains would rise to meet you, a chain of mighty summits that can top 14,000 feet and almost touch the sky.

These are the Rocky Mountains—a towering wilderness of slopes that are impossibly steep, of barren rock faces and frozen tundra. But don't be fooled. Come down to earth and you'll discover that the mountains begin way below the snow peaks. Those rolling foothills and wide river valleys belong to the Rockies as well.

Now you're going to climb them. You're going to sample every stretch of the Rockies—north and south—way on up to their incredible heights. And every step of the way, you're going to experience places alive with animals and plants in spectacular variety.

A Photographic Flight of Fancy:
The Image of A Bald Eagle Set Against a
Rocky Mountain Backdrop

A cloud of red dust billows behind your four-wheel drive vehicle. Before you the mountains are fast approaching. You're at an altitude of 6,000 feet, and still you're in the Rockies' shadow.

The valley you're climbing out of owes its life to the snow peaks. Pull over and peer through your binoculars: The mountains catch the storm clouds. The rain and melting snow run down the slopes to water the prairies below. The grasslands are a gift the Rockies have given to the great herds of American pronghorn.

Notice the way they're huddled? They each face out, ever alert to predators. In fact, their vision is as powerful as your binoculars. For now, though, they're grazing calmly— that is until the still of the mountain air is suddenly broken.

They bolt—at up to 55 miles an hour, almost the speed of your car! Pronghorn are the fastest animals on four legs in all North America. What spooked them?

Then you hear it too: *Wabble doodle! Wabble doodle!*

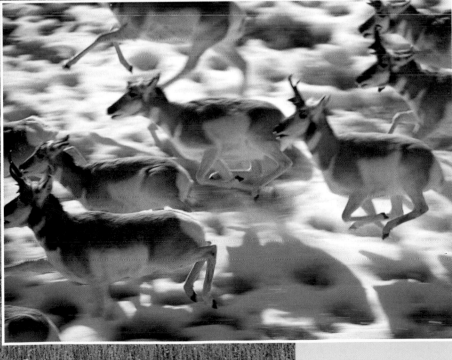

Pronghorn Gallop Through Winter Snow (inset). Pronghorn Grazing in the Foothills of the Rockies (main photo)

5

Just look at those sage grouse chase each other down like a bunch of overgrown roosters. What's all the ruckus?

Wabble doodle!

One male manages to send the others scurrying, and now the crowd stands hushed around him. He proudly struts his stuff, wagging the two hefty air sacks dangling from his chest at every hen in sight. He fans his tail feathers in grand display and puffs out his breast to 25 times its size. This is why he was fighting—to get to stand center stage and perform his crazy mating display. Now he'll be one of the choice few that almost all the females will pick. He's shown he's the strongest, after all, and he'll return every morning for days to prove it again and again in battle.

Across the foothills of the Rockies, courtship is in the air. And new life will soon follow.

A Male Sage Grouse Showing Chest Air Sacks (left inset). Female Sage Grouse Look On (right inset). A Male Sage Grouse's Tail Feather Display (main photo)

6

A Grazing Bison Herd

You've traded in your wheels for climbing boots, and now you pause to catch your breath and gaze below. As far as you can see stretches a herd of that magnificent symbol of the American West.

Once 60 million bison roamed these prairies. Even as Native Americans hunted the animals for food and clothing, they cherished them, and always left plenty alive and well. But over a century ago, the bison were slaughtered by settlers and frontiersmen, until only 23 wild buffalo remained. Now, thanks to conservation efforts, they are returning from near extinction.

Today, they've added one more to their ranks. A new calf struggles to her feet minutes after she was born. But the herd suddenly stands alert. There are shadows amid the sagebrush, awaiting their chance to strike.

A Bison Calf

Coyotes on the Run

You're climbing again, but this time to the top of a cottonwood tree. Behind the cover of leaves you can hide on a makeshift wooden platform, called a blind. In the valley below, the bison gather around the calf to protect her. A pack of hungry coyotes have slipped within the herd. Their goal: to take advantage of any opportunity to get to that calf.

In packs or in pairs, even on their own, coyotes are expert hunters. Alone, they can track a mouse under a foot of snow. Together, they rely on team-work—and the leadership of the top dog of the pack. No one will get to eat without his permission. It's the way of the pack: The top dog rules.

But today, even he'll be going hungry. The pack suddenly flees, leaving the bison calf to trot off with her herd, unharmed. You peer between the leaves of your blind: Other appetites have arrived—another pack of hunters that strike fear even in the coyote.

Up a tree, that's the place to be. Charging in beneath you are the fiercest predators of all the Rockies. With the help of its pack, a wolf can kill an animal 10 times its weight.

Awoooo! They announce it to the world. These mountain woodlands and prairies are their territory, and they're proud of it.

Actually, not long ago they were strangers here. To stop the wolves from killing their livestock, humans nearly wiped them out. Recently, though, conservationists re-released wolves in the wild. In places like Yellowstone, the results were so successful that now wolves are competing with other creatures that share their turf—like coyotes.

Wide as these lands are, the animals who live here are bound to cross paths. Some spread alarm, others an invitation to share their home....

A Wolf Cub (inset).
Wolves at Play (main photo)

13

Kawoosh!—a face full of rapids! Your whitewater raft crashes headlong into walls of water. You're at 7,000 feet, yet still the mountains rise on.

Down a quiet offshoot of your river, the waters take a secret side trip, emptying into a pond. Mallards skim the surface dipping their beaks for insects. An elk pauses for a drink. Who do they have to thank for this paradise?

Bobbing past, four young beaver kits join their parents, busily chewing at an aspen tree. No wonder the river's banks are spreading here. The lodge the beavers are building works like a dam. It's a roomy home, complete with two entrances underwater to protect them from predators. But foe or friend, all animals partake of the pond the beavers have made.

Secreted away in the mountain forest, some animals seek protection—and some seek prey.

Inset photos: Braving the Rapids. A Beaver Nibbling at an Aspen Tree

A Beaver Swims in Front of Its Dam

our heart is pounding. Step by silent step you climb, following the shallow tracks. You can sense you're growing nearer. Now—you freeze. In the still of the mountain forest you feel a pair of eyes upon you.

It was just a glimpse, but there's no question you saw him—and what a privilege that he let you!

Secrecy is the mountain lion's greatest weapon. He can crouch stock still for hours, waiting for a deer or elk to wander by, then leap the length of a school bus to ambush it. He'll make around 30 kills a year and, after each, hide whatever meat is left over to save it for another day.

Many animals in these highland woods must be alert to the mountain lion. Even one of the largest of them all...

A Mountain Lion Licks Her Cub (above). A Mountain Lion Leaping (right)

K-ching, ching go the bear bells on your shoes as you climb on. The last thing a Rocky Mountain hiker wants to do is take a grizzly by surprise—especially when she's guarding her cubs. They're vulnerable to the mountain lion, though he would never mess with a healthy adult grizzly.

She stands eight feet tall and usually weighs almost twice as much as a refrigerator. But after snoozing away the winter, she's lost a fifth of her body weight. Now the whole family is raring to get down the mountain and feast along rivers below, flush with tempting grasses and spawning trout. Your only glimpse of them is their backs, lumbering down the slope.

To what lengths will a mother go to protect her young? Keep climbing and you'll find out.

Grizzly Bear (left). A Mother Bear and Her Cubs Fish for Food (above).

On the way up the mountain, the trees you saw grew taller than a house. Now they've shrunk. Have you entered some strange munchkin world over the rainbow? Yes, in fact, above the tree line. At 10,000 feet, this is a high mountain realm battered by wind and weather.

All winter long, the birds steered clear of here—except for one. The ptarmigan stuck around through the long months of cold. Now she's replaced her snow-white plumage with mottled brown, to blend in with the warm-weather ground cover.

Suddenly a ptarmigan bolts out of the bush. Hurry over, it looks like she's broken her wing! But wait—in a flurry she now flies off and it all becomes clear. She'd been tending to her chicks and, to lure you away from them, she tricked you by pretending to have a broken wing.

Your body is playing tricks on you, too. There's less oxygen at these heights, so you're having trouble catching your breath. The higher you climb, the tougher the Rockies get.

A Ptarmigan in Winter

A Ptarmigan in Summer

The Mountain Tree Line

eep, beep, beep. The pikas scramble, chirping their alarm. The world they live in is called the alpine tundra—a place that's *so cold*, even the soles of their feet are furry.

What else could possibly survive here?

The answer is "plenty." That's the magic of the Rocky Mountains—as you move up the slopes, the habitats change quickly. So within a short distance live many different varieties of life, animal as well as plant.

Past the snow buttercups and the marsh marigolds, through the alpine kittentail and primrose—your path is lined with color. Once a year, even the tundra blooms with wildflowers. Each offers a tempting invitation to view the next. Keep it up, now, you're almost at the top!

A Pika in the Rocks (above).
The Alpine Tundra Blooms (right).

Your every muscle is shaking. You scope out the next crevice in the rock face to brace your ice axe and slam it home. Another six inches conquered. Lucky thing you're roped to the climber above you, because there's nothing but a sheer 200-foot drop below.

But, hey, look there. How do the mountain goats make it look so easy?

They have short, stocky legs, and their hoofs have razor-sharp edges and a rubbery underside to grip the slipperiest ledge. For them, risking these heights is better than risking another animal's appetite. Few predators can follow them up here, so they have the run of the Rockies.

Just a last burst of strength and the summit will be yours. Already the applause is rising to your ears—a thundering clap, echoing across the mountaintops.

A Mountain Goat and Its
Kid on a Rocky Ridge

raaaak! The sound pierces the thin air of the snow peaks. Two male bighorn sheep square off, their massive 30-pound horns crashing in combat. Again and again they drop their heads to slam each other full force. Like the sage grouse, they are sparring to see who'll get to mate. The victor will stand high atop the Rockies to proclaim he alone is the king of the mountains.

But how can he, when up and down these slopes so many animals can make the same claim? Each has earned its crown, whether it's made of horn, feather, or fur.

Two Male Bighorn Sheep Butt Horns (above).
Bighorn Sheep Admire the View (right).

ook around. It's strange—the snow peaks once
so high above, now stretch before you. Peer
down to watch the mountains catch the clouds.
The eagle's domain, a mile in the sky, is now
beneath your feet.

Your gaze wanders with the clouds, across sagebrush prairies and lush river valleys below. Your
imagination soars—on up to highland forests
and summits. To the eagle's skies, to be sure, but
better still, to the slopes she calls home. To all the
wonderful animals living with her high and low
among the Rockies.

Take a deep breath now and tie your hiking
boots tight. For every mountain there's another
adventure awaiting you.

Mountain Goats Traverse the Ridge.

A Note from the National Geographic Society

The Rocky Mountains stretch from New Mexico to British Columbia, almost 2,000 straight-line miles. Some geographers define the Rockies as even longer by including ranges to the north and south. Immense in scope and elevation, the Rockies truly are the "backbone of the continent."

The Rocky Mountains are one of the single most dominant features of the American landscape. They are celebrated in song and American symbol as the "purple mountains majesty" that rise above "the fruited plain." And they are often called "the backbone of the continent." The Rockies are a range of mighty mountains. Geographers usually define a mountain as a landform that rises 1,000 feet or higher above the surrounding area. In Colorado alone, there are more than 50 Rocky Mountain peaks that rise above 14,000 feet. The Rockies' highest summit is Mount Elbert in Colorado. It reaches 14,433 feet.

The Rocky Mountains began forming about a hundred million years ago and continued forming for millions of years. Most are fold mountains—mountains that form when two giant plates forming the Earth's crust collide and compress, or when one of the plates folds and wrinkles due to the collision. When this happens, whole layers of rock can bend, creating beautiful striped patterns in exposed cliffsides. Though the major geological events that formed the Rockies are long over, the Rocky Mountains are still changing shape. Wind, water, and ice act as forces of erosion on the mountains, breaking them down bit by bit, and carving new shapes into the landscape.

Like most tall mountains, the Rockies support several different types of environments, or life zones. Hardy evergreen forest flourishes at the base of the mountains, then gives way to stunted growth above the tree line. Beyond that is the alpine tundra zone. Only specialized plants and animals can survive the cold temperatures, high winds, and limited amounts of water.

People aren't adapted to the cold, harsh, and low-oxygen conditions of the alpine tundra zone, and as altitude increases, it also takes a toll on the human body. But people can survive the alpine tundra zone for reasonable periods of time. It's a challenge many are happy to meet. People are drawn to the mountains and especially to the beautiful Rockies. The Rocky Mountains support many different types of recreation, including hiking, rafting, skiing, snowboarding, cycling, and mountain climbing. People benefit from the natural features of the mountains—the water that runs down from the peaks, the rich ores and minerals that lie within the rock. But too many people enjoying the mountains or overusing their natural resources can put the fragile mountain environment at risk. Wildlife gets edged out by overdevelopment; ecosystems can become damaged or polluted.

A Bull Elk in Rocky Mountain National Park

Conservationists wanting to keep wild lands wild helped form the ten national parks that grace the Rocky Mountains. Here, land and animals are protected and preserved in close to pristine condition, and people can responsibly enjoy the natural glory of the majestic Rocky Mountains.

Alpine primrose blooms in the harsh tundra zone.

The Rockies boast some of the best alpine skiing and snowboarding in the world.

Published by the
National Geographic Society
1145 17th St. N.W.
Washington, D.C. 20036

John M. Fahey, Jr.
President and Chief
Executive Officer

Gilbert M. Grosvenor
Chairman of the Board

Nina D. Hoffman
Senior Vice President

William R. Gray
Vice President and Director
of the Book Division

Staff for this Book

Nancy Laties Feresten
Director of Children's
Publishing

Suzanne Patrick Fonda
Editor

Jennifer Emmett
Associate Editor &
Project Editor

Marianne Koszorus
Design Director of
Children's Publishing

Dorrit Green
Art Director

Janet Dustin
Illustrations Editor

Jo H. Tunstall
Editorial Assistant

Carl Mehler
Director of Maps

Gregory Ugiansky,
Tibor G. Tóth
Map Production & Relief

Lewis R. Bassford
Production Manager

Vincent P. Ryan
Manufacturing Manager

Illustrations Credits

Cover, David Dahms; back cover (up) Howie Garber/STONE; back cover (ctr), Daniel J. Cox/STONE; back cover (lo); John Cancalosi; endpapers, Art Wolfe; 1, James Balog; 3-4 (composite), Darrell Gulin/STONE; 5-6 Tom & Pat Leeson; 6, National Geographic Photographer William Albert Allard; 6-7 (all), Tom & Pat Leeson; 9-10, Ted Wood/STONE; 10, Art Wolfe/STONE; 11-12, Tom & Pat Leeson; 13-14, Tom & Pat Leeson; 14, Daniel J. Cox/STONE; 15 (le), Raymond Gehman; 15 (rt), Tom & Pat Leeson; 15-16, Jen & Des Bartlett; 17, Tom and Pat Leeson; 17-18, Daniel J. Cox/STONE; 19, Daniel J. Cox/Natural Exposures; 20, Tom & Pat Leeson; 21 (up), Tom J. Ulrich; 21 (lo), Raymond Gehman; 21-22, Liz Hymans/STONE; 23, John Cancalosi; 23-24, Kent & Donna Dannen; 25-26, 27, Tom & Pat Leeson; 27-28 Howie Garber/STONE; 29-30, Dean Conger; 32 (up), Art Wolfe/STONE; 32 (lo le), Kent & Donna Dannen; 32 (lo rt), Brian Bailey/Adventure Photo & Film; 33, David Dahms.

To Grace, who's there with me whenever I'm with children—JG

National Geographic would like to thank Dr. Marc Bekoff, a Professor of Biology at the University of Colorado, Boulder, for acting as consultant on this project, Franz J. Camenzind, Ph.D., for reviewing the manuscript and illustrations and providing helpful comments, and William D, Bowman, Ph.D., for his botany expertise and other expert assistance.
The author is grateful to Matt Testa for his research assistance.

FRONT COVER: Mountain Lion
TITLE PAGE: Bighorn Sheep
ENDPAPERS: A Mountain Panorama

Golden Mantled Ground Squirrels Touch Noses in the Rockies.